CAUTIONARY NOTICE TO READERS - DISCLAIMER

Issues related to your Estate Plan are changing regularly. Regulations related to family law, Wills, incapacity and other issues are always under discussion and in a state of change. Financial, tax, corporate succession, risk management strategies, etc. are regularly changing. The author(s), publishers and/or vendors are not providing certified advice. It is recommended that you reference relevant legislation, regulations and tax conventions in your jurisdiction. It is recommended that you seek the professional help of a Certified Financial Planner, accountant and/or estate lawyer before completing your estate plan documents.

ISBN: 978-0-9947836-1-5

Published by Paul Lambe

This project is the sole work of **Paul Lambe CFP FMA**

All efforts were made to make this a proprietary work from past experience, knowledge and research.

Quantity discounts are available for use in educational programs, seminars, workshops, corporate training, college programs, and other initiatives, please contact us by email at estategta@gmail.com.

I

ABOUT THE AUTHOR

Paul Lambe is a currently a Fee-For-Service Certified Financial Planner in St. John's, NL and Ontario, Canada, providing Financial Planning and Estate Management Services.

Paul spent ~20 years in Ontario, Canada as a Certified Financial Planner, serving the Greater Toronto Area.

Paul completed the following educational programs related to finance:

- Certified Financial Planner (CFP) designation in 2000.

- Financial Management Advisor (FMA) program in 2002.

- LUAC- Life and Disability Insurance Level II Licence in 1999 and held this until 2012.

- Post Graduate Marketing Management Honours- Investment Securities Profile, Humber College, Ontario 1992.

- Business and Economics studies Memorial University, St. John's, Newfoundland 1982-1987

Paul has worked as a Financial Planner since 1996, with several large financial services companies in Canada, providing advice and wealth management services to meet the financial goals and needs of clients.

Paul was a self-employed financial and estate consultant for executors, trustees and POAs from 2012-2015 and has returned to this business in 2018.

Paul enjoys reading/research/writing, playing soccer, playing golf, mountain climbing, hiking, travel, culture and history.

Paul climbed Mt. Kilimanjaro, Tanzania in 2004 to raise funds and awareness for ALS.

Paul accomplished 'A Mountain for Maddie' in 2008, climbing Mt. Elbrus, to help fund Free the Children initiatives of Maddison 'Maddie' Babineau. Maddie passed at 15 while raising funds to build a well in an African village, for which she gave her Children's Wish to build a school.

THE ESTATE PLAN WORKBOOK

Paul Lambe

TABLE OF CONTENTS

INTRODUCTION

Estate Planning is the process of arranging your personal affairs. It involves the transfer and management of assets when a person dies, becomes disabled or incapacitated, or chooses to have someone else manage their affairs.

I have spent most of the last twenty years working closely with clients and other professionals in the financial planning industry, especially on client's estate planning. I assisted clients in settling estates with and without estate plans in place, and can tell you it is much easier on everyone with an estate plan in place.

It is believed in industry circles that as many as 50% of the adult population do not have an estate plan in place. Some of the reasons for this are; people find the topic morbid, people not wanting to engage a lawyer and/or other professionals, or the cost and time that needs to be put into it.

It is because of this I discovered the need for <u>The Estate Plan Workbook</u>. A tool you can work on yourself at your own pace, fill in your specific details at the back of the book, let your wishes be known and get them down on paper.

You will establish your wishes to be included in your Will, you will determine your wishes related to your personal care and health, you will determine your wishes on how your property is to be managed, as well as other important decisions you may need to make. This is the hardest part for most people, so once this is done you can have your Certified Financial Planner review it, and then have the proper documents drafted by a lawyer. I will repeat the need to consider professionals many times in the book.

There are many do-it-yourself options out there also if you decide to go this route after completing this workbook.

This book is a tool, workbook and a guide to help you get your wishes on paper. Our objective is to keep it as simple as possible for the average person to understand the aspects of an estate plan.

This book does not give legal or tax advice but merely points out important issues in these areas. After completing this workbook, a lawyer should be able to complete drafting your documents with relative ease saving you money on legal fees, versus going through a complete estate planning process. In more complex situations you will see that you may need to discuss those issues with your Certified Financial Planner first and/or with a lawyer.

It is said that 'Estate Planning is The Process of Living and Dying Neatly'. Besides creating a descriptive Will through your estate plan, your affairs while you are alive are also addressed, and then drafted into legal documents in case you cannot manage your affairs for some reason.

Our objective in this workbook is to help you pull together most of your wishes and choices for your estate plan as it exists at this point in time. Each section will deal with a specific part of your estate plan development.

You may realize through this process that there are gaps in your estate plan that you may need to take care of with the help of professionals; a Certified Financial Planner, an accountant, and/or a lawyer.

Wills, trusts, powers of attorney/advanced health care directives/living wills, gifting, tax planning, beneficiary designations, joint ownership, corporate succession issues and risk management are all common tools used in estate planning and you can determine if they are necessary for you.

We will explain important concepts of the estate plan so you get a basic understanding of the various parts. You can then go to a section at the back to fill in your wishes and notes. It is advisable to read the full book first then go through the workbook section, and refer back to the table of contents and reread sections that apply to you. I have purposely not included an index or a glossary to keep the workbook simple, and to recommend you reread sections completely when necessary.

The Estate Plan Workbook is not a complete Estate Planning Guide, it is an introduction to estate planning. It is more for those who need an introduction to Will planning, personal care and property issues. It is for single people, the young family, couples, people with investment assets, insurance, a home and personal property who wish to organize their estate properly.

We will discuss common strategies and concepts in Estate Planning, however it is outside the scope of this book to provide detailed estate planning. You should work with your Certified Financial Planner, accountant and/or lawyer on complex estate planning issues that involve more complicated trusts, business assets, blended families, more than one real estate property, substantial investment assets, and assets in multiple jurisdictions.

My objective is to also provide information relevant in most common law jurisdictions. Common law jurisdictions include those where many of the laws are from precedents, previous legal decisions usually made by a judge, court or tribunal. Common law jurisdictions include Canada (ex Quebec), UK, US (ex Louisiana), etc.

I personally believe that the effort I have put into this workbook will help many people get their affairs organized and on paper.

Paul Lambe CFP FMA, 2014

1.

PROBATE AND ADMINISTRATION OF AN ESTATE

Probate is a process used to confirm the validity of a Will and the appointment of the executor, estate trustee or personal representative to act on behalf of the deceased or the estate. The executor/estate trustee can use the resulting authority given in this document(s) to settle the estate and transfer property to the named beneficiaries of the estate.

In the case there is no Will, the next of kin can apply for letters of administration which will confirm the legal authority of the applicant as the administrator to act on behalf of the estate and distribute property to next of kin.

The process of probate requires filling out forms and submitting them to the appropriate body in your jurisdiction, usually a court which then issues letters probate, letters of administration, letters of authority, letters testamentary, a certificate of executor or estate trustee, etc. These give legal authority to the applicant to deal with the administration of the estate through third parties such as financial institutions, government institutions, bill payees, and any entity that may require a grant of probate.

In most jurisdictions (i.e. state, provincial) the government provides access to rules and forms and you can research how the process works. Completing the probate process individually is possible for most people, however, it can be challenging at times especially with more complex assets, structures or wishes of the deceased.

Small estates, which can be defined differently in many jurisdictions, can often be settled without probate.

Probate is often required when assets are held individually, for example a savings account – the financial institution will often freeze the account when advised of the death of the owner and probate may then be required to access the funds.

- Many financial institutions allow certain payments from these accounts such as payment directly to a funeral home.
- Sole ownership of a property may also require probate
- Probate can be required when there is no named beneficiary on assets, such as registered assets and life insurance proceeds.
- Probate can be required when there is a wrongful-death proceedings or minor dependents

Probate fees, estate taxes or death taxes? Fees or 'taxes' owing can vary depending on your jurisdiction and the size of your estate. It may not be required where all transfers of assets are completed outside of the estate. Some jurisdictions have a minimum estate value before fees are charged, others charge a flat fee on the total value, i.e $15 per $1,000, or 1.5%, so on a $1 million estate, this can result in probate fees of $15,000 payable by the estate.

Methods of reducing probate fees? Probate fees can be reduced by employing some of the options below. Probate fees can be relatively small compared to income tax due on death, executor/estate trustee fees and/or legal fees.

- Changing assets or property to joint tenancy with your spouse, children, or other intended recipients can provide a direct transfer of assets and avoid fees. However, this may create problems such as loss of control over assets, capital gains on the change, or creditors or spouse of your joint owner making a claim.

- If you do not have a need for the assets, you can give or gift the property to your intended recipients prior to an estate.
- You may be able to name secondary or alternate beneficiaries on registered plans and insurance policies in case your primary beneficiaries predecease you or die in a common disaster with you.

It is advisable to review your estate plan with a Certified Financial Planner to discuss probate issues, and ascertain if employing these strategies are necessary or not.

2.

INTESTACY – DYING WITHOUT A WILL

Without a Will, the deceased's assets are distributed according to his or her jurisdiction's intestate succession law. The rules of intestacy are inflexible, and may not be in accordance with the deceased's wishes.

Intestacy can create many issues for your successors;
- Your estate may be distributed in a manner you had not wanted. Usually your next of kin would inherit according to the Table of Consanguinity which details blood relationships. (See Table of Consanguinity below.)
- A person may have to apply to the court to be appointed the administrator of your estate, or a government agency may become the administrator if no person applies.
- A person may have to apply to the court to be appointed the guardian of minor children.
- The court may appoint a guardian for children who may not be the person you may have chosen.
- Access to assets may be restricted until an administrator is named, the estate is settled or children reach the age of majority.
- Your spouse may not inherit everything you wish, as many jurisdictions split assets between spouse and children.
- A business could be left in an indeterminate state for a period of time.
- If in a second marriage you may unintentionally disinherit children altogether.
- A common-law spouse or partner may not receive what you may have intended.

- Family or children outside of wedlock may or may not receive what you intended.
- If you die without a spouse or blood relative the government may inherit.

a) Table of Consanguinity

Table of Consanguinity

This table can be used in intestate cases to determine who is in line to inherit from the 'Person' deceased. From Person you go down the column, children would inherit first, if no children then Grandchildren would inherit, if no Grandchildren, then Great-Grandchildren.

If none of the above are living, then we go to the second column and start with the Parents of the 'Person', the deceased. We go down this column until there is an heir(s).

If no heir(s) is determined in the second column, continue to the top of the third column, and so on.

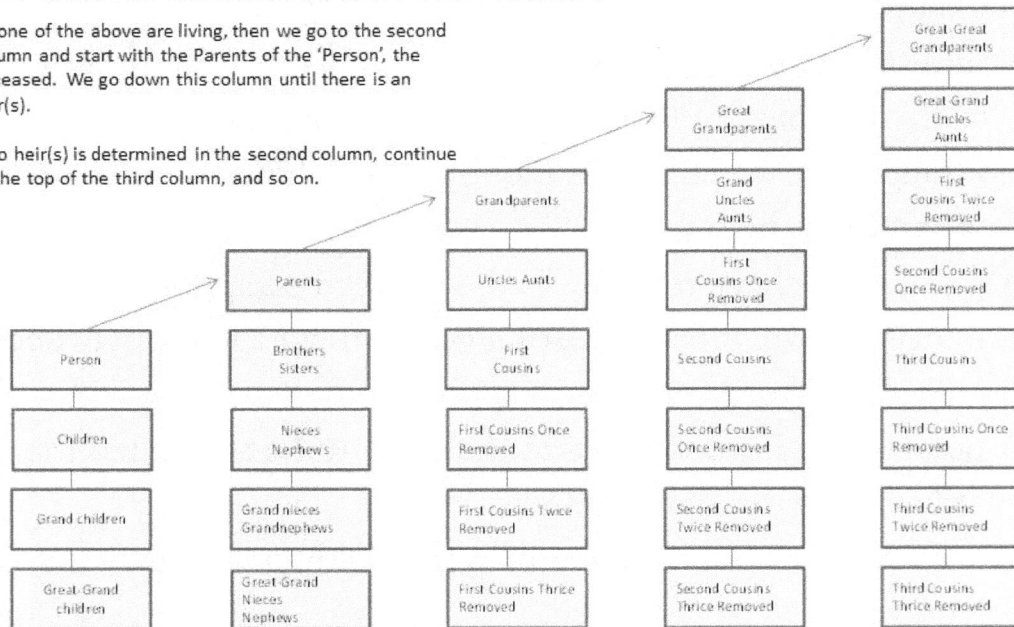

Person	Parents	Grandparents	Great Grandparents	Great-Great Grandparents
	Brothers Sisters	Uncles Aunts	Grand Uncles Aunts	Great-Grand Uncles Aunts
Children	Nieces Nephews	First Cousins	First Cousins Once Removed	First Cousins Twice Removed
Grand children	Grand nieces Grandnephews	First Cousins Once Removed	Second Cousins	Second Cousins Once Removed
Great-Grand children	Great-Grand Nieces Nephews	First Cousins Twice Removed	Second Cousins Once Removed	Third Cousins
		First Cousins Thrice Removed	Second Cousins Twice Removed	Third Cousins Once Removed
			Second Cousins Thrice Removed	Third Cousins Twice Removed
				Third Cousins Thrice Removed

Created by Paul Lambo FMA. It is important to consult with an expert when it comes to intestacy and consanguinity

For any and all of these reasons, it is very important for you to get your wishes together, create a Will and instructions for Personal Care and Property.

3.

YOUR LAST WILL AND TESTAMENT

A Will, also known as a Last Will and Testament, is the cornerstone of any properly structured estate plan. A Will or Testament is a legal document that, if properly executed declares a person's final wishes. The person who creates the Will, the testator (male) or testatrix (female), names one or more persons known as an estate trustee, executor/executrix, personal representative or liquidator to manage the distribution of the estate property to chosen beneficiaries, and carry out any other final wishes.

Issues commonly dealt with are whether some assets will be held in trust, at what age minor children will receive their inheritance, who will act as guardian of minor children, how your affairs can be structured to minimize income taxes, probate fees, succession duties, inheritance taxes and if desired funeral and\or burial instructions. These are just some of the many questions which are addressed in the preparation of a Will.

The best time to prepare a Will is immediately. Many people neglect it for too long, others leave it until they hear of someone else's dire situation, when a domestic contract such as a cohabitation, marriage or separation agreement requires the parties to make a Will, and others before a trip or major surgery who are forced to make decisions very quickly.

You and your spouse, common-law spouse or partner should have your own Wills and should discuss and be familiar with the requirements of each other's Will. A Will can be a joint Will as in a husband and wife Will where the parties involved make very similar or identical provisions. These have also been known as a mirror/mutual/reciprocal Wills in many jurisdictions.

Any person over the age of majority and being of sound mind can create a Will with or without the use of a lawyer. A lawyer should always be considered if there is a complicated issue, such as a large estate, if there is a change in marital status, if any assets are held outside of your current jurisdiction, or if there is a question of capacity, etc.

There is no legal requirement that a Will be drafted by a lawyer, however it is highly recommended to avoid problems, as the person will not be around to clarify. As an example, some jurisdictions can disinherit a beneficiary named in the Will who acts as a witness regardless of the provisions of the Will.

A Will names a person's beneficiaries/divisees/legatees - those who are to receive the person's property.

A properly executed Will in many jurisdictions is signed at the end of the document by the testator in the presence of two witnesses who are not beneficiaries.

Many jurisdictions recognize holographic Wills, which are handwritten by the testator. A holograph Will is completely written by hand and signed by the testator. Holographic Wills do not need to be witnessed in most jurisdictions, and can be probated with minimal requirements. It should be dated but not required.

Holographic Wills can provide complications for the estate trustee/executor by not having enough detail or instruction. They are only appropriate where the estate is minimal or in emergency situations where someone needs to leave last minute instructions and wishes.

a) Items to Prepare or Consider for Your Will.

i)   Estate Goals

The first step is to decide on goals for the remainder of your lifetime, and prepare for them, as well as what you want to do with your estate when you die.

You may want to:

- leave a neat estate, with as much detail as possible so that your executor has great direction and detail, your wishes are well documented and your beneficiaries are provided for as you wish
- leave a suitable estate for your spouse, children or grandchildren (i.e. through life insurance?)
- provide for a child or adult who has a physical or mental impairment (i.e. in a trust)
- minimize or defer estate expenses and income tax
- transfer your business effectively to a family member or other (i.e. complex planning)
- leave specific personal items to selected people, specific legacies or bequests (i.e. mother's ring to daughter)
- donate to your desired charities
- make your funeral wishes known (i.e. burial or cremation?)
- make your organ donation wishes known (i.e. to a university for science or specific organs only?)

ii)   Personal Information

Besides your name and address, information related to your family and also historical information should be provided.

iii) Financial Information

Your assets and liabilities should be provided to determine the appropriate detail of your Will and possible planning opportunities.

iv) Revocation Clause

You should revoke all previous Wills that were created before the date of the new Will through a clause in the Will.

v) Appoint an Estate Representative

An Estate Trustee/Executor, Personal Representative or Liquidator should be appointed in your Will. This person or trust will be responsible for distributing the property according to the terms of the Will. We will use executor, estate trustee, or representative interchangeably to refer to these in the workbook.

It is very important to take the necessary time and consideration to choose an appropriate executor as this person will be charged with the task of carrying out your final wishes. You may appoint more than one person to act as executor if the estate is complicated or you prefer to have two working together. You may want to indicate if they should act jointly or severally.

- Joint executors often have to work together and sign together.
- 'Several' appointees can act independently, in a separate or individual way.

It is also a good practice to name an alternate executor in case the person(s) cannot act.

To make a good choice please consider the following:

1. Choose someone you can trust.
2. Consider someone who is competent, has knowledge related to executorship and/or can manage with appropriate help.
3. The person(s) should not be someone who would have a conflict of interest.
4. Financially proficient, can understand and account for financial matters.
5. Consider the persons age and health, you do not want someone who may predecease you.
6. Do not think that a relative is always the appropriate choice; you need someone who will look out for all beneficiaries as you will indicate.
7. Consider an executor in your jurisdiction. Executors from outside your jurisdiction may have to post bond, or there may be restrictions.
8. Consider naming two children if they are adults to avoid any resentment with favoring one child over the others.
9. Speak to your possible executor first to determine if they would be willing.
10. Consider someone who is capable of carrying out any and all of the following tasks and possibly more:
    - Search for your Will
    - Arrange reading of the Will
    - Secure your residence, assets and any other property
    - Arrange for funeral and /or burial if directed
    - Get death certificate(s)
    - Compile an inventory and a list of assets and liabilities
    - Cancel subscriptions and services
    - Delete internet profiles

- Arrange for probate and paperwork to be completed
- Search for next of kin and legitimate heirs
- Estimate taxes owing and holdback funds until confirmed
- Advertise for creditors
- Satisfy bequests and legacies
- Inform government agencies and financial institutions
- Collect debts owing and pay debts owed
- Arrange for consolidation, distribution and/or sale of assets. Home and contents, cottage and contents, business, investments, bank accounts, etc.
- Deal with insurance contracts
- Apply for death benefits
- Gather and review previous tax details and file appropriate tax returns
- Deal with estate legal matters, i.e. file lawsuits or defend against them.
- Assure heirs and beneficiaries of proper accounting, distribution and timelines
- Get income tax clearances
- Get releases from beneficiaries

Consider letting your family know what your Will says and who you have chosen so it can limit any future arguments.

Consider giving your executor a copy of your Will and estate plan in advance to help them with their obligation.

If you cannot find someone you know, then consider professional help. There are options available for a professional agent to help an executor, as I do, or options for professionals to act as your executor for compensation, i.e. lawyers or trusts.

Estate administration and licuidation can be a complex process involving a lot of research, transactions and paperwork. Each estate settlement is different in complexity. Consider the time, effort and capability required.

Even if an estate is relatively straightforward, it can take between one and two years to be fully administered and distributed.

Other professional services may be required such as real estate maintenance, legal, investigative or genealogical/heir research, etc.

vi) Powers for Executor/Estate Trustee to Act

The Will should also provide the executor or the trustees with wide powers to invest, manage and sell property, to borrow, to lend, to make income tax elections, to pay debts and expenses, to forgive loans, power to retain agents and advisors for assistance - at his/her discretion. The executor or trustees may be subject to jurisdictional rules and not be able to take advantage of all options available if these powers are not included. (See following Trust section for more information on **'Powers of Trustees'**.)

vii) Guardian(s), Conservator and Custody

A guardian, conservator or protector should be named for minor children or an incapacitated dependent, also known as a ward. Those named can become 'Legal' when appointed or approved by a court.

It is important that a legal guardian or guardians be named in the Will as your choice to be granted custody of a child or children. Custody usually has to be confirmed by a court order.

The legal guardian should also be given guardianship of property for minor children. If the parents die before children reach the age of majority, they can manage this property appropriately for the benefit of the children.

Guardians et al have a legal responsibility to the 'person' (child) for the daily care, upbringing and decision making related to health care, education, religion, activities, etc. Responsibility for 'property' may fall under other regulations, and it is usually recommended that provisions and instructions be provided in a Will for a trust to deal with property. Without a Will a child may be entitled to receive the estate upon attaining the age of majority, which most experts consider to still be too young to receive considerable assets. (See following '**Trusts for Minors;**' section under Trusts.)

Parents do not usually have to be appointed as legal guardians, and a surviving parent becomes guardian if they have been cohabiting or they share custody. It can be suggested that if you are separated or share custody that you make the other parent the guardian in writing in case something happens and to avoid another relative from applying for guardianship for some reason. If both parents die, a legal guardian will have to be appointed. A parent with sole custody who does not want the other parent as guardian should seek legal advice, as most parents would be appointed unless the court rules he or she is unsuitable.

In choosing an appropriate guardian you should consider those who:

- would have a similar parenting style, share the same values and religious beliefs
- capable of taking on the care of a child, financially, physically and emotionally
- is very familiar to your child, or is a close family member

Many jurisdictional courts make or confirm the final decision on who will be the legal guardian of minor children. Parent(s) should state their preference in the Will as it would be very persuasive in any proceedings.

Guardians for incapacitated or the mentally handicapped adults also have to follow jurisdictional procedures to be appointed legal guardian.

People can name more than one guardian if deemed necessary, and also name an alternate in case the others for some reason do not or cannot accept the responsibility.

You also have the option to provide specific instructions in your Will to your chosen guardian on religious beliefs, cultural preferences or other items that provide more relative guidance for your guardian in future decision making. You may also want include instructions on health care matters such as medical treatments for your children, however you may want to discuss these in advance with your physician or child's physician.

You should also include details on compensation for guardian(s), or detail how you feel about this.

viii) Beneficiary(s)

Beneficiaries are the people or entities you name in your Will to receive a benefit from your estate or those you name on a plan, account, policy or trust.

A residual beneficiary is a person or entity who shares in the residue of the estate after all other obligations have been met, including the payment of debts, taxes, expenses and bequests/legacies have been honored.

A testamentary trust beneficiary is a person or entity you have indicated will receive a benefit from your estate, but it will be held in a trust. A trust does not have to be a complicated entity; the simplest form of testamentary trust can be created by indicating at what ages minor children are to receive their inheritance. It is recommended that more details be given for a trust for minors indicating how funds will be paid out over time or accessed by trustees for their benefit.

It is a good idea to also name alternate or contingent beneficiaries in case the primary beneficiary(s) predecease you, dies in a common disaster with you, or in rare cases declines to receive the assets.

Beneficiary designations on certain investment plans or accounts as well as insurance policies are usually done with the provider and not duplicated in your Will unless there is a good reason for it. Most providers make sure you fill this out on signup or on changes.

Many jurisdictions protect the rights of a spouse and/or dependents to a share of the estate, even if they are not named as beneficiaries.

ix)   Bequests/Legacies/Devise(s)

A bequest and a legacy are often used interchangeably. However, a bequest is usually when someone gives personal property and a legacy is usually when someone gives money to a person or charity through their Will. A divise is a clause giving real property, land or real estate through a Will.

If you want to leave a family heirloom, china collection, in-kind donations to a charity or foundation, or any specific item to a specific person or organization you would include it as a bequest. For example, 'I bequeath my mother's wedding ring, to my daughter Elizabeth.'

It is important to leave enough detail about the bequest/legacy/devise so that the item or amount is easily identified or determined. For example, 'I would like to leave a legacy of exactly $10,000 to my friend William _____.'

A bequest or legacy can be made conditional on an event or situation. i.e. 'provided William is neither incarcerated nor incapacitated'.

Bequests/legacies should be reviewed to ensure they are still applicable over time.

Ademption occurs when a bequeathed asset is no longer in the estate. The gift to the beneficiary fails and there is no other entitlement.

Abatement occurs when there are not enough funds to satisfy a legacies or gifts, so a proportional reduction has to be made.

Charitable bequests or legacies:

It is very important to be very clear when making a gift to a charity as it is their duty to ensure it has received its intended donation. A charity my request a review of the administration of an estate if the details of the donation is not clear such as if they are a residual beneficiary, meaning the proper administration of the estate can determine what their entitlement is. If you leave a specific dollar amount to a charity you can easily avoid these issues. For example, 'I would like to leave a legacy of exactly $10,000 to my favorite charity The Favorite Charity in city, province/state, country, registration #11111111.'

Charitable bequests have tax benefits in most jurisdictions.

Another way to indicate who should receive items is a personal property memorandum. By referring to it in your Will you may make it legally binding in many jurisdictions. You can list the tangible personal property items, the person you would like to receive each item and then sign it. It does not usually need to be witnessed. It can be used if you have many items to list for a number of people. You should keep and update this with your estate documents. It is also a good idea to openly communicate your wishes.

x)   Proper Maintenance and Support to Spouse and Dependents

The Will should provide direction with respect to providing adequate support to spouses, children or other dependents.

Regardless of what is written in the Will, most jurisdictions have laws that dictate a spousal share, homestead rights and methods for dependents to apply for support payments.

xi) Trusts

In simplest terms in common law legal systems, a trust is a relationship whereby property is held by one party, the trustee, for the benefit of another, the beneficiary.

Trusts are frequently created in Wills, defining how money and property will be handled for children or other beneficiaries. The Will may establish the terms of any trusts to be created upon death.

Many people consider trusts to be a vehicle for the wealthy and to manage complicated affairs. However, this is not really the case. An example of a trust in the simplest of uses in a Will is, 'I leave all my assets in trust for my children.' With this the executor or estate trustee can set up a trust for the children. The trust will be managed according to the jurisdictional rules, however this can lead to many problems and complications, i.e What if there are claims by children born outside of wedlock? When can assets like a house/the home, land, cottage, or cabin be sold? etc. See the powers you can give your trustees below to add substance and direction to this trust or similar.

The reasons for settling a trust are numerous, however trust legislation and taxation are constantly changing in many jurisdictions and it is outside the scope of this workbook to provide anything but an introduction to trusts.

From this introduction you will get an idea on how trusts can work. We will explain some of the most popular uses for trusts in estate and tax planning, family planning, and providing for minors or disabled beneficiaries.

A trust is created by a settlor, who transfers some or all of his or her property to a trustee. The trustee holds that property for the trust's beneficiaries. A trustee can be a person, a company or a government body. There can be a single trustee or multiple co-trustees.

An owner placing property into a trust turns over the property's legal ownership and control to the trustee(s). This may be done for tax reasons or to control the property and its benefits if the settlor is absent, incapacitated, or dead.

The trustee is obligated to act for the good of the beneficiaries. The trustee may be compensated and have expenses reimbursed, but otherwise must manage income and trust property for the beneficiaries benefit.

Common responsibilities of the trustee:
- Prudently manage and invest the trust property;
- Avoid conflicts of interest;
- Act with an even hand towards beneficiaries, treat all equally, unless stipulated in trust document;
- Avoid improper delegation of authority;
- Inform beneficiaries of their entitlements;
- Sell trust property as required;
- Pay the trust's debts and taxes.

The trust is governed by the terms under which it was created. In most jurisdictions, this requires a contractual trust agreement, deed or a properly drafted Will.

For a trust to be valid in most jurisdictions it must show three certainties:

1) Certainty of Intention: it should be clear that the donor or settlor intends to create a trust
2) Certainty of subject matter: it should be clear what property is to be part of the trust and each beneficiaries interest can be defined
3) Certainty of objects: it should be clear who the objects, or beneficiaries are

There are two main types of trusts, *Inter vivos* or living trust, and testamentary trust.

(i)   Inter vivos trust or living trust:

A settlor who is living at the time the trust is established creates an *inter vivos* trust or living trust.

Some common uses of living trusts:
- Provide income to children of a previous marriage or relationship
- Provide income to an ex-spouse based on a divorce or separation agreement
- Manage assets for someone who lacks financial expertise
- Manage assets and/or income for a disabled or incapacitated person
- To hold or manage a gift to minors
- Tax planning opportunities (Constantly changing)
- To provide future gifts or donations to charities
- Avoid probate, estate fees and/or taxes

- To keep asset information confidential

(ii)   Testamentary Trusts

Testamentary Trusts are created in Wills; in fact, most properly drafted Wills have all of the dispositions with respect to the estate and the distribution of the estate done on a trusts basis.

Testamentary trusts allow for three main things:
1) Income splitting,
2) Control beyond the grave,
3) Creditor protection of the beneficiaries.

Some common uses of testamentary trusts:
- Provide for a minor beneficiary
- Provide income or living interest to a surviving spouse
- Manage assets for beneficiaries who lack financial expertise
- Manage assets and/or income for a disabled or incapacitated person
- Manage assets for a spendthrift or incarcerated person
- Tax planning opportunities (Constantly changing)
- To provide future gifts or donations to charities

Testamentary trusts are also used to hold property such as a home or cottage for the benefit of a number of beneficiaries for a period of time. It is important to leave funds available for maintenance, repairs, property taxes and other expenses related to this type of property.

(iii) Trusts for Minors:

A testamentary trust can be used to hold property for the benefit of minor children until they reach the age of majority or later. The trust should give the trustees discretion to invest and provide income or capital to the guardians of the children to pay for ongoing expenses for care, for educational or recreational programs, and for opportunities for the children.

Testamentary trusts should be used to postpone the ultimate receipt of property from an estate until children or grandchildren have reached a more mature age than simply the age of majority. This ensures that the children on reaching the age of majority are not given a large sum or assets that they may not know how to manage properly.

Trustees can be given the power to pay for any post-secondary education, lump sum for a wedding, a car, a down payment, etc. The trustees can be given the power and task of winding down the trust when the child is a mature adult and/or capable of managing the remaining funds. You can choose an age or various ages for lump sum distributions, you can choose a partial distribution each year of income and/or capital, up until a specific age for final division or distribution of all assets, or you can leave it to the discretion of the trustees to determine a time.

Similar trusts can be created for the other common uses mentioned above, with specific instructions for each situation.

(iv)   Powers of Trustees

All trusts can give or expand the powers of the trustees to act. It is important to give careful consideration to these powers to allow the trustees to act flexibly in administering the trust assets.

- Investments - Some jurisdictional rules can be restrictive to trusts. Give the trustee(s) discretionary or broader powers to invest in 'prudent' assets that are considered practical for the administration of the trust over time.
- Payments from trusts - The trustee can decide on paying debts and expenses, paying out all or partial income to beneficiaries, and also encroaching on capital as required.
- To sell and/or retain assets – business shares and real estate assets require wide-ranging rules to be managed properly - to carry on the business, to incorporate other assets, to manage assets as a shareholder, etc.
- Borrow or lend money – loans to beneficiaries at preferred rates, borrow until assets are sold, renew or continue debt obligations, management of mortgages on trust property, etc.
- Make income tax elections – trusts are often set up for tax purposes, rules vary in each jurisdiction and trustees should be able to make income tax decisions.
- Entitlement to compensation – to pay trustees according to local guidelines.
- Retain and/or employ agents and advisors – experts and/or professionals may be required for complicated or specific tasks.

You may wish to research these uses for inter vivos or testamentary trusts, and if they can be used in your jurisdiction:

Insurance Trust – A trust is named to hold the proceeds of an insurance policy for beneficiaries.

Offshore Trust – Can be used for gifts or inheritances from non-residents, or for immigration.

Irrevocable Trust – cannot be amended, retracted or wound down without the permission of the beneficiary(s).

Spousal Trust – Can be created in a Will to provide maintenance or support for surviving spouse.

It is advisable that a person seek professional help from your Certified Financial Planner and/or estate lawyer on estate planning using trusts.

xii) Failure or a Common Disaster Clause

Failure or common disaster refers to the situation where spouses, partners and/or beneficiaries die at the same time, or within a short period of time. If they are named as each other's beneficiaries there can be complications if there isn't such a clause. (For example, in a car accident spouses are seriously injured and die within a few days of each other. Usually the person's estate who died second will inherit all from the person who died first, then his or her beneficiaries will inherit all.) You can include, in the event of failure or common disaster, each of the person's alternate beneficiaries would inherit. It may be important to include a number of days where a spouse or partner has to survive you by, i.e. 30 days.

xiii) Divorce and Beneficiaries

In some jurisdictions you may want to state that any part of your estate (and its growth in value) that your children inherit will be separate from their family property. A child could have a divorce immediately following your death and end up losing one half of the inheritance to the ex-spouse. Your lawyer can give you further advice on this point.

xiv) Posting Bond or a Surety

To protect an estate, and executor or estate trustee may be required to post an estate administration bond, or provide a surety. A bond can be an insurance policy to protect the estate and beneficiaries from fraud or wrongdoing. A surety is usually a person who assures the executor will complete tasks as indicated by putting up assets. An executor may be relieved from posting a bond by submitting a valid request to court. Bonds are often required for an executor from outside the jurisdiction of the assets.

xv) Executor Liability Clause

This provides protection for an executor from being sued. i.e. By beneficiaries if an investment loss occurs and the executor has broad investment discretion. If assets are complex - market values can regularly change, liquidation may take time, and there are often limited things an executor can do at times.

xvi) Executor Compensation

Executors should be compensated for their time and effort. Consider a 'gift', a fee or a percentage indicated in the Will.

xvii) Children Born Outside of Wedlock

Children may be treated differently depending on jurisdiction. i.e. Old English rules often exclude children and/or other relatives born outside of wedlock. More recently many jurisdictions treat them as equal beneficiaries to other children. It is important that your Will expressly details your wishes.

xviii) Exclusion of a Person(s) from your Will

If you choose to exclude someone who would be considered a beneficiary or next-of-kin from your Will it is important to explain why in detail. It can reduce the possibility of arguments or any challenges to the Will later.

b) Funeral Arrangements

Making funeral arrangements in advance, or at least discussing your wishes with family members, will relieve them of having to make these decisions after your death.

One good reason to do it in advance is the cost, last minute services are usually marked up, and it's not a good time to be shopping around, making emotional decisions. Pre-made arrangements which can be paid for later are often a good idea. Most funeral homes provide seminars so you can enlighten yourself on the choices beforehand, and shopping around early always helps. Funds can be placed in a trust fund to pay the costs later. The contract may be cancelled later and other arrangements made if desired. If you do prepay, get a copy of the contract, signed by both parties and detailing the items requested and the costs and terms associated.

A life insurance policy can also be purchased so that funds are available to cover funeral costs. This is an ideal option for young people, single people, those with limited funds available, or anyone else who can arrange reasonable premiums. Insurance can be available through many funeral service providers; however it may be better to get a personal insurance agent or see your Certified Financial Planner to arrange.

The manner in which a person can have their remains dealt with and the costs can leave family members in a difficult position in making decisions and agreeing.

You should list directions in your Will as to what funeral arrangements should be carried out if not already arranged. (i.e. cremation, burial, location, etc.)

- Earth burial is the usually the body being placed in a coffin or casket and buried in the ground in the traditional manor, covered in soil. Some people have skipped the coffin, and have been buried in just a shroud.
- Cremation is the burning or combustion of the body to ashes. Cremation is an alternative to burial and the ashes may be buried, interred or dispersed as per wishes.
- Body donation to science. Many medical schools accept anatomical donations, often cover the costs associated with retrieving the body, and returning cremated remains to the family.
- There are other choices. Some people want environmental options, others want more economical options, so you should make note of your customs, culture and beliefs related to your funeral and the processes you wish carried out.

Cremation has become a popular choice over the last half century or more as it can save money, and it can be simpler. You can have the body cremated and then spread the ashes over a place of choice or kept in an urn avoiding the cost of a casket and plot.

If you have decided to make an anatomical gift of your body to an institution, you should include instructions in case the donee declines for some unknown reason. You should also include your instructions for a ritual or memorial service.

Memorial societies exist in many jurisdictions to help find simpler and cheaper options in an increasingly expensive funeral services market. They help members plan and arrange for funeral or cremation without the pressure of providing an extravagant funeral.

Do it yourself options do exist in many jurisdictions. You can buy your own casket or even a shroud, have a family member arrange to receive and transport the body, get death certificates or permits, deliver to a crematorium or burial plot, and arrange a private memorial service. It is wise to get estimates on all options.

Some costs and considerations associated with burial decision;
- Transportation of the body from place to place
- Casket
- Embalming and/or cosmetic restoration and services by funeral home
- Vault or Grave liner
- Viewing service and facility
- Ritual service
- Grave plot
- Open and closing grave
- Transportation of mourners
- Clergy fee

- Obituary fees
- Copies of death certificate
- Music
- Flowers

Some costs and considerations associated with cremation decision;
- Transportation of the body from place to place
- Viewing service and facility
- Casket for service
- Crematorium charges and container
- Urn and and/or plot (Columbarium)
- Ritual service
- Transportation of mourners
- Clergy fee
- Obituary fees
- Copies of death certificate
- Music
- Flowers

It is often recommended that funeral arrangements be left in memorandum form so they can easily be accessed before the Will is read.

You can fill in our detailed section on funeral instructions, then sign it, let your executor or family know where it is, and have your lawyer review if you wish to make it legal.

It is wise to review the funeral and burial laws of your jurisdiction while planning. There are often laws and regulations related to who can or will be responsible for your funeral and burial, where you can be buried, where ashes can be spread, whether embalming is required, and dealing with funeral homes and mortuary contracts.

c) Body or Organ Donation

Make your wishes known on how you feel about body or organ donation.

There are many reasons to donate your body or organs. Everyone should consider themselves potential donor no matter your age or medical history. Even if your organs can't be used, it's likely that you can be a tissue donor, giving anything from corneas to heart valves to a needy recipient. Your complete body can be donated to a university or medical school for research purposes or you can choose to donate only what you choose, for example, eye banks are one of the oldest organ donation options. So make sure to give organ donation serious thought.

Many possible body and organs that could be donated are not because potential donors didn't make their families aware of their wishes which lead to many people, who are waiting for an organ transplant, continuing to suffer or pass away.

If you're interested in donating your organs after you pass on, or if you want to make that decision for your family, there are steps you should take to ensure that it happens. Most jurisdictions have their own rules for body and/or organ donations so it's best to inform yourself of the rules. There are donor cards or a designation on your driver's license; you may contact a local university or medical school or you can also create a memorandum for organ or body donation so that it is available immediately.

While a signed donor card and a driver's license with an "organ donor" designation are legal documents in most jurisdictions, it is during the window of opportunity i.e. in a hospital on a ventilator, that the next-of-kin will give the approval that you intended to be a donor. The timeline for organ donation is immediately after death.

So, it is very important that you discuss your wishes with your family and/or your executor/estate trustee beforehand, as the Will may not be read for days after death.

As organ donation can depend on the condition of your organs, body, etc. it is also advisable to indicate in the memorandum or in your funeral instructions (just in case) what is to be done if they are not accepted due to delay, an autopsy is required, poor condition, or other reason. The donee has the right to decline, and may not have the resources to deal with non-usable organ donations.

d) Witnesses to the Will

All Wills except holograph Wills should be witnessed by two people. The witnesses should not be a spouse or a beneficiary named in the Will.

It has been suggested that the signor and both witnesses initial each page of the Will and then sign/witness the signature page to protect against insertions of pages in the Will later.

It may be an important consideration at the time of witnessing to get an affidavit sworn and signed by one or both witnesses identifying the Will and attesting that they witnessed your signature on the Will. This may save time and effort when the estate trustee or executor has to have the Will validated or probated and will need this affidavit. Significant delays in probate can occur if witnesses cannot be found or are deceased and there is no affidavit.

e) Revising your Will

A Will should be revised after any of these occurrences,

- Divorce, separation or cohabitation. Most jurisdictions consider income and property acquired during the marriage as family property, which is usually equally divisible amongst spouses. Some jurisdictions include common-law and same-sex partners, it is advisable to check your jurisdiction's legislation.
- Change in status of a beneficiary or executor. If someone predeceases you, an executor moves out of jurisdiction, a revision may be in order.
- A child reaching age of majority. Children reaching age of majority have full access to any inheritance, if you do not wish this, you may consider a trust to spread the inheritance out over time, and include conditions.
- A change in jurisdiction, province/state/country. Most jurisdictions have different legislation.
- Assets acquired in another jurisdiction, or you can create another Will in that jurisdiction for those specific assets only.
- Disposition of specific or significant assets named in the Will. You do not want your executor searching for assets that do not exist, and/or beneficiaries questioning where assets named in a Will are.

Most changes to a Will can be done using a codicil, which is an amendment to the Will and can contain information on any addition, explanation or modification of anything in the Will. The codicil will need to be signed and witnessed as with the original Will, however the witnesses need not be the same, and it is a good practice to get an affidavit to the signature again.

f) Memorandums

A memorandum is an expression of wishes which can be added to your estate documents. Most estate trustees or executors will accept it as additional direction from the Will, but it is not usually legally binding. It is important to discuss with a lawyer in your jurisdiction how to make it legally binding.

Besides the personal property memorandum mentioned under bequests, where you list the names of beneficiaries for tangible personal property such as heirlooms, art, vehicles, etc., you can use memorandums for other purposes.

- A memorandum for digital assets is a good idea, this can contain all of your user names/identifications/IDs and passwords for accessing an account.
- You should also consider a memorandum for funeral instructions so that it is available immediately on death to those who need to make the arrangements, instead of waiting for the Will to be read.
- You can also use a memorandum for organ donation to express your wishes if you have not made other arrangements, and make sure it is accessible to family members immediately when needed.

A Will is a very important and powerful document and you should think seriously about what you put into it. This section has explained most of the more common choices you have to make.

There may be other items you may need to include in your Will or under a clause. Take note of any issue we may not have covered to discuss with your Certified Financial Planner and estate lawyer.

4.

PERSONAL CARE AND PROPERTY DECISIONS

a) Power(s) of Attorney/Authorizations et al

Power(s) of Attorney, Living Will, Health Care Authorization, Health Care Proxy, Health Care Directive, Health Care Consent, Health Care Power of Attorney, Substitute Health Care Decision Maker, Advanced Health Care Directive, Advance Medical Directive, etc.

These are all written authorizations to represent or act on another's behalf with regard to wishes and/or decisions of a personal nature while that person is alive. The person authorizing the other to act can be known as the donor, grantor or principal. The one authorized to act on the donor's behalf can be the attorney, donee, grantee, conservator or proxy. This person can act under this authorization only while the person is alive, once a person dies the Will determines what must be done and the executor/estate trustee takes over.

Everyone should have these authorizations in place. Think about your family circumstances and finances if tomorrow you were unable to make decisions. Who is capable and who do you trust to make these decisions for you?

Your jurisdiction will most likely refer to one of the above, in most common law jurisdictions in Canada you would have Power(s) of Attorney, POAs, for personal care and property, in some US states you could have a Healthcare Proxy or a Healthcare POA added to a Living Will to create an Advance Medical Directive. These are not all the same and some jurisdictions have considerable differences. Our purpose is to help you get your wishes related to these authorizations on paper and then you can have a lawyer in your area review and draft them according to your jurisdictional rules and definitions.

We will use Powers of Attorney (POAs) for (1) Personal Care and (2) Property to explain these concepts so you can get an understanding of decisions you can make and what you should have in place while you are alive, to give as much guidance as you wish. The person(s) authorized may have to make very important and sometimes difficult decisions related to your personal care or your property.

The purpose of these authorizations is to have someone act on your behalf, if you choose to have them do it, or you are unable to do something yourself. You may be unable to act on your own because of health reasons, being out of the jurisdiction, or some other reason. It is important to give them as much instruction as you can.

If there is no POA in place for a person or it is not valid after incapacitation, the person may become a ward of the jurisdiction. A family member or another party would most likely then have to apply for guardianship, conservatorship, or such.

b) Personal Care Decisions

A power of attorney for personal care will give someone the authorization to act on your behalf with respect to your personal care, such as making medical, health care, shelter, nutrition, clothing, safety and hygiene decisions for you, or act on your personal instructions that are in the document related to these decisions.

Medical and healthcare decisions - Some of the choices that you or your POA may have to make if diagnosed with a terminal or a progressive incapacity illness are to accept or refuse these treatments:

- Life Support - refers to emergency treatment to sustain life after the failure of one or more organs.
- Intubation - refers to an inserted tube that can be used to provide food to those who cannot feed themselves or cannot swallow. It can also be used to assist in breathing and administering drugs.

- Cardiopulmonary Resuscitation (CPR) - is usually performed on someone who is in cardiac arrest. It involves chest compressions and artificial ventilation in an attempt to restore the heart and lungs to natural working order.

- Do not resuscitate (DNR) - is a legal order written by a doctor or included in your POA to prevent resuscitation in the event of cardiac or respiratory arrest.

You or your POA may also have to make decisions on the following:
a) Shelter – Where you will live, in your own home or in a care home?
b) Nutrition – How and when meals will be provided.
c) Hygiene – How and how often you will be washed.
d) Clothing – What to wear, how and when to change.
e) Safety – How you will be kept safe from things or people that may cause harm.

c) Property Decisions

A power of attorney for property will allow someone to manage your property, financial assets and belongings.

Under a general power of attorney - your attorney, donee, grantee, or proxy can manage your real estate and investments (including selling, buying, mortgaging), pay your bills and expenses, file your tax returns, and sign most documents for you.

In most jurisdictions it is important that you comply with the following in designating a POA for Property:
  o You as donor should be at least the age of majority.
  o You must be mentally capable.
  o You as donor should be aware of all property owned and its approximate value.

o   You as donor should be aware of your jurisdictional financial obligations to dependents.
o   You as donor should be aware of all that your attorney has the authority to do.
o   You as donor should be aware of what accountability the POA has.

d) Choosing a Power of Attorney

To whom should you give these authorizations to carry out your wishes?

You should choose an adult, above the age of majority in your jurisdiction who is:

- Mentally capable of making sensible decisions
- Trustworthy, has been honest in all dealings and you have known a long time
- Financially proficient, can understand and account for financial matters
- Objective, or not easily influenced by personal feelings or opinions in representing your wishes

This person can refuse the request to act for you, so it is important to ask this person if they will accept the responsibility to carry out any and all of your wishes. It would not be wise to have someone who may resign the appointment and leave you in a state of limbo or an indeterminate state.

You can have two persons named, but you should dictate whether they have to act together (jointly) on all decisions, or if they can make decisions together or separately (jointly or severally). Jointly can be a safeguard against fraud by one person as they have to make unanimous decisions. However, a process for resolving disputes should then be provided to get past stalemates by joint POAs.

You can also name a substitute, who can act for you in case the original(s) cannot.

e) Types of Power of Attorney

What types of Powers of Attorney can you create?

General or Limited

- General POA can give significant authorizations over some or all of your legal and financial decisions while you are mentally capable. It can be for a specific period of time i.e. while in hospital or while an asset is being sold (home, cottage, business), and it can end if you become incapacitated.
- Limited General POA will give more specific authorizations, and/or for a specific period of time.

In the past, most general or limited POAs were revoked on incapacity, giving rise to the following more durable POAs.

Enduring, Continuing and Springing POAs

- Enduring POA is one that authorizes your attorney to continue to act for you if you become incapable, it is also known as a 'POA with durable powers', 'Durable POA' and 'Continuing POA'. It can take effect immediately if necessary.
- Springing POA usually comes into effect on a specific date, event or after incapacity.

You can indicate in the document what should be done to determine or substantiate your incapacity, such as a friend, capacity assessor, family doctor or specialist's affirmation or certification. Sometimes two doctor's certifications can be required.

f) Duties of a POA

What the attorney cannot or should not do in most jurisdictions?

A POA cannot replace you in some fiduciary capacity such as a director of a company, as an attorney under someone else's power of attorney, as an executor/estate trustee of another's Will or a as trustee.

A POA does not have to or should not act in the best interest of the family of the donor, grantor or principal. The POA should always act in the interest of the donor and their wishes. However the POA may consult with family for help in making a decision.

A POA cannot or should not:
- Make any change to or revoke a Will of the donor;
- Modify a beneficiary designation;
- Delegate his or her responsibilities to another;
- Donate the donor's property;
- Benefit personally from carrying out the responsibilities of the power of attorney, outside of reasonable compensation;
- Allow a conflict of interest with the wishes of the donor.

g) Who does the POA Account to?

- The donor at any time can request an accounting;
- A monitor can be appointed in the power by the donor to receive an accounting at certain time intervals, i.e. once or twice per year or on request;
- Anyone authorized by jurisdictional law may make an application or request for an accounting.

Also:
1. A power of attorney should document and keep an accounting of all transactions.

2. Keep the donor's financial assets and property separate and apart from his or her own finances and property.
3. An attorney should be prepared at all times to justify his or her decisions as sound on behalf of the donor and keep good notes.

h) Assets in Multiple Jurisdictions

It is important to consult with an estate practitioner in all jurisdictions where property is held in order to determine what inclusions should be made in the jurisdiction where the document(s) are drafted.

i) Assets in a Jurisdictions with a Different Language

It is important to consult with an estate practitioner in all jurisdictions where property is held and a different language is used in order to determine inclusions that should be made.

j) POA Compensation

Do you feel your attorney should be compensated for the time and effort put into carrying out your wishes?

Your jurisdiction may have recommendations or rules for what compensation can be paid to your power of attorney.

k) Other Notations on POA/Authorizations:

- You have to sign and date these authorizations; however you should consider having two witnesses to your documents. Rules related to number of witnesses and who should be a witness can vary in jurisdictions, so check your requirements.
- You should discuss your options and decisions with your family doctor, and request a final copy to be filed in your physician's medical file.

- You should consider giving copies to a family member or be sure they are readily accessible if needed.
- You should discuss your choices with those closest to you so they are clear on how you feel about these issues.
- Consider giving your agent/POA – authority and discretion to gather and share personal health information governed by legislation with third parties.
- Some jurisdictions still do not recognize a POA/Living Will until a person is diagnosed as terminal.

Use the workbook section at the back to fill in your wishes. If your wishes are extensive and/or complicated you should consult an estate lawyer to help with decisions and review before drafting your documents.

5.

ESTATE PLANNING CONSIDERATIONS

There can be many other considerations and decisions for individuals and families to make outside of those already discussed such as Wills, Trusts, POAs, etc.

Estate Planning options are available in all jurisdictions and can be very complex if your family situation is complicated, and/or you have significant assets. We will touch on some ideas in this section, but it is recommended that if they apply to you, to seek the professional help of a Certified Financial Planner, accountant and/or estate lawyer.

a) Designating Beneficiaries on Qualified Accounts and Plans

Beneficiary designation can be made on most retirement accounts, registered assets, pensions, insurance policies/contracts, and trusts.

Possible reasons for beneficiary designation:
1) Easier transfer of assets
2) Avoidance of probate
3) Tax strategies, deferral or reduction

- Designating minors as beneficiaries may create problems, as the jurisdiction may hold assets in trust until the age of majority, and then the beneficiary would receive all. This may still be too young to manage considerable assets.
- Some jurisdictions have rules protecting spousal rights as a beneficiary.

- Keep beneficiary designations up to date on your accounts and plans, as the most recent designation should prevail. Be careful not to make a conflict in your Will with designated beneficiaries on accounts and plans.

b) Joint Ownership

When property is owned by two or more people it is considered jointly owned.

1) Joint Tenants - have the right of survivorship, so the assets usually pass directly to the survivors and avoid probate and estate fees or taxes.

2) Tenants in Common - usually do not have the right to survivorship. So the deceased's share of the property would pass through their estate to their beneficiaries, who could become a joint owner, or the property is sold.

It is important to determine which type of joint ownership you would like and make sure details are included in the ownership agreement as some jurisdictions treat joint tenancies and tenancies in common the same.

Problems with joint ownership can include:
- Loss of control – asset(s) are managed by all owners
- Exposure to creditors of joint owners
- Triggering of capital gains
- Reporting of future income

A common alternative to joint ownership is an inter vivos trust.

c) Taxation

Taxation is very different in most jurisdictions, and if tax savings are a large part of your estate planning objectives then you will need to see a professional as it is outside the scope of this workbook. It is advisable to consult with a qualified Certified Financial Planner and accountant, who are known experts in taxation in your jurisdiction.

Some considerations for your jurisdiction(s):
1) Capital gains tax and elections
2) Spousal rollovers
3) Dependent rollovers
4) Charitable contributions
5) Trusts

Trusts for instance historically had clear tax advantages; however legislators are constantly changing the rules as they search for more tax revenue sources.

d) Life Insurance

Life insurance can be the simplest method of providing for and protecting an estate.

- If you have little or no assets and wish to provide funds for your dependents or beneficiaries. i.e. If you are single and do not have the funds to pay for your own funeral, then life insurance can be the best option. A basic life insurance policy of $100,000 can help pay for funeral expenses and have funds left over to help out surviving family members.

- If you have minor children you may need a larger policy to pay for their expenses until they reach the age of majority. You may also want to provide for their post-secondary education.

- You may want to provide for payment of the mortgage, imagine leaving your spouse as a single parent caring for children alone. If funds are not there to cover expenses they may be forced to sell the home.

- Life insurance can also be left in a life insurance trust with payments made over a period of time to named beneficiaries.

    o Life Insurance Trusts

    Life Insurance trusts can be created by making the designation within the policy or plan. i.e. My brother William _____ in trust for my children. The terms and powers of the trust can then be written into the Will.

See your Certified Financial Planner, or a licensed insurance agent to discuss various options for your situation, including types of life insurance and premium options.

e) Gifting

Gifting or giving assets to family prior to passing can avoid possible problems for the estate and ensure the appropriate people have the assets. You can see the difference you make as they use them while you are alive. i.e. Consider a gift of money each year before a special time or event, birthday, anniversary, holiday, it can allow all to enjoy the event more.

With gifting assets such as investments or real estate, there are issues to consider like triggering capital gains, future needs, and giving up control. i.e. Passing the family cottage may create a capital gain, however, future gains appreciate to the new owner. Capital losses may be able to be used through gifting of capital assets.

Making donations to charity – many charitable donations during life and after death to a charity come with tax benefits.

f) Multiple Wills

There are some situations where multiple Wills should be considered.

- Assets in another jurisdiction – it is often easier for an estate to be settled if there is a Will written in the jurisdiction of the property owned.

  Different jurisdictions have different tax rules, probate and legal considerations. i.e. How would a property transfer or sale in Florida or the Bahamas be handled? What if there was a divorce or marriage?

  In some foreign jurisdictions it can make sense to hold the property or assets in a trust with named beneficiaries for a less complicated transfer.

- Business assets and succession –you may have a separate Will to transfer the shares or ownership of a business outside of probate. Considerations related to these business interests are outside the scope of this workbook.
  1. Proprietorship – Sole owner
  2. Partnership – Share of partnership
  3. Incorporated – Share(s) of corporation
     a. Transfer the shares to family members

b. Sell the shares to partners, shareholders, employees, or third parties

c. Wind up the business and sell assets

g) Final Considerations on Estate Planning

- Determine how much immediate cash may be needed to pay bills on passing. Keep it in an accessible account for the estate representative.

- Keep an updated net worth statement each year with details on your assets and liabilities.

Get your estate in order now, to ease the burden for family.

7.

APPENDIX - PERSONAL WORKBOOK:
GET YOUR WISHES ON PAPER

Fill in as much detail in each area with your wishes and notes. Refer back to the appropriate chapter when you need to review terms.

Cut out this section if you wish. Make a copy of this section for your spouse/partner, and also a working copy.

Any areas you are not ready to complete, skip and continue on, you may return to them later.

a) Estate Goals

Examples:

- Leave a neat and detailed estate
- Leave a suitable estate
- Provide for a dependent
- Minimize estate fees and tax
- Legacies or bequests
- Donate to charity
- Make your funeral wishes known
- Make your organ donation wishes

1) _____

2) _____

3) _____

4) _____

5) _____

6) _____

Additional notes on your estate wishes:

_____

_____

_____

_____

_____

b) Personal Information

- Fill in information on lines provided.
- Use margins for notes if necessary, as more detail is always constructive.

Your name

_____

Date of birth and place of birth

_____

Occupation

_____

Address

_____

Telephone (Home) (Work) (Mobile)

_____

Email

_____

Spouse, common-law or partner name

_____

Date of birth and place of birth

_____

Occupation

_____

Address

_____

Telephone (Home) (Work) (Mobile)

_____

Email

_____

Marital Status

Single   Yes ___ No ___

Married   Yes ___ No ___

Common-Law or partner (_____)   Yes ___ No ___

Divorced or separated   Yes ___ No ___

Previous - spouse, common-law or partner name

Name

_____

Date of birth and place of birth

_____

Jurisdiction of marriage

_____

Date of divorce   _____

        Jurisdiction of divorce _____

Marriage or domestic contract?   Yes ___ No ___ (Provide copy)

Divorce, separation agreement or court order?   Yes ___ No ___ (Provide copy)

Your citizenship _____

Spouse/partner citizenship _____

Domicile or Permanent Home

_____

Previous marriage by either spouse   Yes ___ No ___

Whom? _____

Child support, alimony or other obligation?

_____

Location of any documents related to previous marriage, child support, alimony or any other obligation

_____

Children from current relationship:

Name   Date of birth

_____   _____

_____   _____

_____   _____

_____   _____

_____   _____

_____   _____

Children from a previous relationship:

Name   Date of birth

_____   _____

_____   _____

_____   _____

_____   _____

_____   _____

_____   _____

Are any children disabled?   Yes ___ No ___

Name   Nature of disability

_____   _____

_____   _____

_____   _____

_____   _____

_____   _____

_____   _____

Are there any other dependents?   Yes _____ No _____

Name   Relationship   Reason for dependence

_____ _____   _____

_____ _____   _____

_____ _____   _____

_____ _____   _____

_____ _____   _____

_____ _____   _____

Grandchildren:

Name   Date of birth

_____   _____

_____   _____

_____ _____

_____ _____

_____ _____

_____ _____

Parents (Indicate if deceased) Name(s)

_____

Phone Number(s)

_____

Address(s)

_____

Parents of spouse (Indicate if deceased)
Name(s)

_____

Phone Number(s)

_____

Address(s)

_____

Location of any documents related to dependents

_____

Notes:

_____

_____

c) Medical Information

Personal Physician Name

_____

Phone Number

_____

Address

_____

Spouse, common-law or partner Personal Physician Name

_____

Phone Number

_____

Address

_____

Location of any documents related to above information

_____

Specialist Physician Name (s)

_____

Phone Number

_____

Address

_____

Spouse, common-law or partner Personal Physician Name

_____

Phone Number

_____

Address

_____

d) Property and Financial Information

i) Income information

Current annual income

Employment _____   Business _____

Rent   _____   Royalties _____

Pension   _____   Other   _____

Other   _____   Other   _____

Notes on income sources: (i.e. Pension, business, rental details)

_____

_____

_____

_____

_____

_____

ii) Asset Information

1. Real Estate Properties (location and value)

Home

_____

Is this a Matrimonial Home?   Yes _____ No _____

Cottage

_____

Investment property

_____

Foreign property

In whose name is the real estate if other than you?

_____

_____

2. Personal Use Property: (Approximate Value)

Valuables such as jewelry, paintings, heirlooms, china, gold, silver, coins, china, memorabilia, etc.

Item name   Approximate Value

_____   _____

_____   _____

_____   _____

_____   _____

_____   _____

_____   _____

_____   _____

Personal use items not listed above (i.e. vehicles, boat, ATV, cabin, land?)

                                    Approximate Value

Automobile   _____

Automobile   _____

Boat   _____

ATV   _____

Cabin   _____

Land   _____

Other   _____

Other   _____

Household goods -   Approximate Value

Furniture   _____

Machinery	_____
Tools	_____
Equipment	_____

3. Financial Institution(s) Accounts (Savings, checking, safety deposit.)

Financial Institution(s) name & address

_____

Account Holder(s) _____ _____

Financial Institution(s) name & address

_____

Account Holder(s) _____ _____

Safety deposit box (location and in whose name?)
Financial Institution(s) name & address

_____

Account Holder(s) _____ _____

If you have more than one financial institution, please copy these pages.

4. Individual Non-Registered Investment Assets

Financial Institution(s) name & address

_____

Type	Market Value	Adjusted Cost Base
Stocks	$ _____	_____
Bonds	$ _____	_____
ETFs	$ _____	_____
Mutual Funds	$ _____	_____
GICs	$ _____	_____
Bank Accounts	$ _____	_____

Other _____ $ _____   _____

Other _____ $ _____   _____

Other _____ $ _____   _____

Other _____ $ _____   _____

5. Joint Non-Registered Investment Assets

Financial Institution(s) name & address

_____

Type	Market Value	Adjusted Cost Base
Stocks	$ _____	_____
Bonds	$ _____	_____
ETFs	$ _____	_____
Mutual Funds	$ _____	_____
GICs	$ _____	_____
Bank Accounts	$ _____	_____
Other _____	$ _____	_____
Other _____	$ _____	_____
Other _____	$ _____	_____
Other _____	$ _____	_____

6. Retirement, Pension or Registered Investment Accounts

(RPP, RRSP, Education Plan, 401K, etc.)

Financial Institution(s) name & address

_____

Type	Face Value	Beneficiary (s)	Account held with
_____	$ _____	_____	_____
_____	$ _____	_____	_____

_____	$_____	_____	_____
_____	$_____	_____	_____
_____	$_____	_____	_____
_____	$_____	_____	_____
_____	$_____	_____	_____
_____	$_____	_____	_____
_____	$_____	_____	_____
_____	$_____	_____	_____

7. Business Ownership Interests

Company name   Ownership percentage

_____   _____

_____   _____

8. Life Insurance Policies

Policy number	Type of coverage (Term 10, UL, etc.)	Beneficiary (s) (Named on policy)	Insurance Company
_____	_____	_____	_____
_____	_____	_____	_____
_____	_____	_____	_____
_____	_____	_____	_____
_____	_____	_____	_____
_____	_____	_____	_____

Location of policies

_____

_____

9. Debts Owing to You by a Third Party

Name   Details

_____   _____

_____   _____

_____   _____

_____   _____

10. Inheritance

(To Come? From whom, from where, relationship, amount?)

_____

_____

_____

_____

Location of any documents related to above assets

_____

_____

_____

_____

vii) Liabilities

Mortgages

_____   _____

_____   _____

_____   _____

_____   _____

Loans, credit card balances, other debts.

Type   Amount   Holder of debt

(Financial Institution)

_____   _____   _____
_____   _____   _____
_____   _____   _____
_____   _____   _____
_____   _____   _____
_____   _____   _____
_____   _____   _____
_____   _____   _____

Location of any documents related to above liabilities

_____
_____
_____
_____

viii) Other Items of Note: (Location, number, details)

Safety deposit box key,

_____

Post office box key/number

_____

Other keys

_____

Combination locks

_____

Safe combination

_____

Hiding place for items

_____

Burglar alarm code(s)

_____

Copyrights, patents, trademarks

_____

Tax records are held

_____

Court judgement pending

_____

Additional notes on any of the above items of note:

_____

_____

_____

_____

_____

_____

_____

_____

_____

e) Digital Account Information

Attention: This section's details especially should be kept in a very safe place. i.e. Safe or safety deposit box.

Devices, email, internet accounts, accounts/cards and memberships – Identification (ID), passwords, PINs, etc. (Fill in as much as known.)

Digital devices – i.e. phone, desktop, laptop, notebook.

Device _____

     User ID _____ Password _____

Device _____

     User ID _____ Password _____

Device _____

     User ID _____ Password _____

Device _____

     User ID _____ Password _____

Mobile Device 1 _____

     User ID _____ Password _____

     Voicemail: _____

Mobile Device 2 _____

     User ID _____ Password _____

     Voicemail: _____

Virtual Private Network (VPN) - Name _____

     User ID _____ Password _____

Locked files or folders -   Name _____

     User ID _____ Password _____

Disk or file encryption details

_____

_____

Email accounts

Email 1- Provider (i.e. hotmail.com) _____

      User ID _____ Password _____

Email 2- Provider (i.e. hotmail.com) _____

      User ID _____ Password _____

Internet accounts

Facebook

      User ID _____ Password _____

LinkedIn

      User ID _____ Password _____

Twitter

      User ID _____ Password _____

MySpace

      User ID _____ Password _____

Instagram _____

      User ID _____ Password _____

Other _____

      User ID _____ Password _____

Other _____

      User ID _____ Password _____

Other _____

      User ID _____ Password _____

Codes, passwords and PIN numbers

ATM card 1   _____

ATM card 2   _____

ATM card 3   _____

Garage door   _____

Credit card   _____

Credit card   _____

Alarm system   _____

On-line trading   _____

Other   _____

Other   _____

Other   _____

Other   _____

Other   _____

Do you use password management software?   Yes ___ No ___

    Details:

_____

Location of any documents related to above information

_____

Other items of note:

_____

_____

_____

_____

f) Professional and Personal Contacts

Certified Financial Planner/Broker/Advisor - Name

_____

Phone Numbers

_____

Address

Lawyer – Name

_____

Phone Numbers

_____

Address

_____

Personal Banker/ Name

_____

Phone Numbers

_____

Address

_____

Employee Benefits Representative - Name

_____

Phone Numbers

_____

Address

_____

Insurance Agent/Auto/Home/Marine/Umbrella - Name

_____

Phone Numbers

_____

Address

_____

Insurance Agent/Auto/Home/Marine/Umbrella - Name

_____

Phone Numbers

_____

Address

_____

Next of kin - Name

_____

Phone Numbers

_____

Address

_____

Clergy Name

_____

Phone Numbers

_____

Address

_____

Other - Name

_____

Phone Numbers

_____

Address

_____

Other - Name

_____

Phone Numbers

_____

Address

_____

Other - Name

_____

Phone Numbers

_____

Address

_____

Other - Name

_____

Other - Name

_____

Other - Name

_____

Other - Name

_____

Other - Name

_____

Other - Name

_____

g) Instructions for Your Will

Where will you keep the original copy of your Will?

_____

Please refer back to 'Your Last Will and Testament' section as often as necessary to make sure you enter the correct information and add detail to the 'Notes' sections.

Do you revoke all previous Wills that were created before the date of the new Will?

Yes __ No __ Date of new Will? _____

i) Executor/Estate Trustee/Liquidator(s):

Name: _____ Relationship: _____

Name: _____ Relationship: _____

Address(es) of Executor/Estate Trustee/Liquidator (s):

_____

_____

ii) Alternate Executor/Estate Trustee/Liquidator(s)

(If initial predeceases you or is unable to act):

Name: _____ Relationship: _____

Name: _____ Relationship: _____

Address(es) of alternate Executor/Estate Trustee/Liquidator(s):

_____

_____

iii) Special Executor/Estate Trustee/Liquidator Provisions

(ie: Foreign Executor/Estate Trustee/Liquidator for assets in another jurisdiction?)

_____

_____

iv) Powers for the Executor et al

Powers for the executor/estate trustee/trustee, liquidator or personal representative(s) to manage assets.

Give careful consideration to these powers to allow the trustees to act flexibly in administering the trust assets. (See **'Powers'** in Trusts section.)

- Investments   Yes __ No __
- Payments from trusts   Yes __ No __
- To sell and/or retain assets   Yes __ No __
- Borrow or lend money   Yes __ No __
- Renew or maintain debt obligations   Yes __ No __
- Retain and/or employ agents and advisors   Yes __ No __

v) Executor/Estate Trustee et al Compensation   Yes __ No __

'Gift' or a specific fee or percentage.

_____

_____

_____

_____

vi) Bequests

(i.e.: jewelry, art, individual personal items or articles, family heirlooms):

You can choose to create a Personal Property Memorandum instead with a detailed list of items and for whom. If you wish to do this see Personal Property memorandum at the end. Refer to it in your Will.

If you have only a few specific bequests, list them here.

Please list your specific bequests

Name: _____

Bequest: _____

Name: _____

Bequest: _____

Name: _____

Bequest: _____

Name: _____

Bequest: _____

Name: _____

Bequest: _____

Name: _____

Bequest: _____

Name: _____

Bequest: _____

Name: _____

Bequest: _____

Name: _____

Bequest: _____

vii) Cash Legacies:

You may leave specific cash amounts to people or charities in your Will provided there will be cash available in the estate after-taxes.

Name: _____

Legacy: _____

Name: _____

Legacy: _____

Name: _____

Legacy: _____

Name: _____

Legacy: _____

Name: _____

Legacy: _____

viii) Exclusion(s)

Explain why a person or persons were excluded from the Will. It can reduce the possibility of arguments later.

Name: _____

Explanation: _____

_____

_____

Name: _____

Explanation: _____

_____

_____

ix) Estate Residue:

Distribution of Estate Residue after bequests and legacies are complete:

Primary beneficiary(s) – please indicate relationship (i.e. spouse, father, mother, sister, brother, etc.)

Name: _____   Relationship: _____

Name: _____   Relationship: _____

Name: _____   Relationship: _____

Name: _____   Relationship: _____

Name: _____   Relationship: _____

Name: _____   Relationship: _____

If spouse and/or children and a trust(s) to be created.

Provisions for a Spouse ((including financial support, and when spouse will receive income, capital, and/or full distribution from any trust)?):

Notes:

_____

_____

_____

_____

Trustee(s):

Name: _____   Relationship: _____

Name: _____   Relationship: _____

Name: _____   Relationship: _____

Provisions for Children (including financial support, and ages at which they receive income, capital, and/or full distribution from trust):

Notes:

_____

_____

_____

_____

Trustee(s):

Name: _____   Relationship: _____

Name: _____   Relationship: _____

Name: _____   Relationship: _____

x) Powers for the Trustee(s)

(Trust Name 1 _____)

Give careful consideration to these powers to allow the trustees to act flexibly in administering the trust assets. (See **'Powers'** in Trusts section.)

- Investments   Yes __ No __
- Payments from trusts   Yes __ No __
- To sell and/or retain assets   Yes __ No __
- Borrow or lend money   Yes __ No __
- Renew or maintain debt obligations   Yes __ No __
- Entitlement to compensation   Yes __ No __
- Retain and/or employ agents and advisors Yes __ No __

Powers for the Trustee(s)

(Trust Name 2 _____)

Give careful consideration to these powers to allow the trustees to act flexibly in administering the trust assets. (See **'Powers'** in Trusts section.)

- Investments   Yes __ No __
- Payments from trusts   Yes __ No __
- To sell and/or retain assets   Yes __ No __
- Borrow or lend money   Yes __ No __
- Renew or maintain debt obligations   Yes __ No __
- Entitlement to compensation   Yes __ No __
- Retain and/or employ agents and advisors Yes __ No __

Alternate beneficiary(s) **Failure or Common Disaster** - if none of above beneficiaries are alive or if all die in common accident:

Name: _____ Relationship: _____

Name: _____ Relationship: _____

Special instructions: (i.e. Number of days you predecease person)

_____

_____

Trustee(s):

Name: _____ Relationship: _____

Name: _____ Relationship: _____

Powers for the Trustee(s)

(Trust Name 3 _____)

Give careful consideration to these powers to allow the trustees to act flexibly in administering the trust assets. (See **'Powers'** in Trusts section.)

- Investments   Yes __ No __
- Payments from trusts   Yes __ No __
- To sell and/or retain assets   Yes __ No __
- Borrow or lend money   Yes __ No __
- Renew or maintain debt obligations   Yes __ No __
- Entitlement to compensation   Yes __ No __
- Retain and/or employ agents and advisors Yes __ No __

Divorce - related to beneficiaries: (Separate property?)

Notes:

_____

_____

_____

_____

Children outside of wedlock:

Notes:

_____

_____

_____

_____

xi) Guardianship:

Guardian(s):

Name   Relationship

_____   _____

_____   _____

Address(es) of Guardian(s):

_____

_____

Alternate Guardian(s):

Name   Relationship

_____   _____

_____   _____

Address(es) of alternate Guardian(s):

_____

_____

Special Guardian Provisions: (Notes on health care matters such as medical treatments, religious beliefs, cultural preferences, compensation or other items that provide more relative guidance for your guardian in future decision making.)

_____

_____

_____

_____

_____

_____

_____

_____

_____

_____

_____

_____

xii) Will for Assets in Another Jurisdiction

It is important to have a separate Will for assets in other jurisdictions, made in that jurisdiction.

Do you have assets in another state, province or country?   Yes __ No __

Do you have a separate Will for these assets?   Yes __ No __

_____

_____

h) Funeral Instructions

It is a good practice to get information on funeral options and costs associated.

Cost and consideration estimates associated with burial decision: (From your research)

- Transportation of the body from place to place _____
- Casket _____
- Embalming or cosmetic restoration and services by funeral home _____
- Vault or Grave liner _____
- Viewing service and facility _____
- Ritual service _____
- Grave plot _____
- Open and closing grave _____
- Transportation of mourners _____
- Clergy fee _____
- Obituary fees _____
- Copies of death certificate _____
- Music _____
- Flowers _____

Cost and consideration estimates associated with cremation decision:

- Transportation of the body from place to place _____
- Viewing service and facility _____
- Casket for service _____
- Crematorium charges and container _____
- Urn and plot (Columbarium) _____
- Ritual service _____

- Transportation of mourners _____
- Clergy fee _____
- Obituary fees _____
- Copies of death certificate _____
- Music _____
- Flowers _____

How will your funeral be paid for? (i.e. funds from estate, insurance policy, prepaid details, etc.)

_____

_____

My thoughts as to my funeral related to customs, culture and beliefs, traditional funeral or an informal gathering:

_____

_____

Have you made funeral arrangements? Yes ____ No ____

Funeral Provider Name

_____

Phone Number _____

Address

_____

_____

Do you own a cemetery plot and have you arranged for ongoing care and maintenance?

Yes__ No__

_____

Have you prepaid for your funeral?   Yes ___   No ___

If you have not made arrangements:

Do you wish to be cremated or buried? Cremated _____   Burial _____

Earth burial, mausoleum entombment, cremation, inurnment, internment, grave, crypt, niche, other details?

Are instructions in your Will or elsewhere? Yes ___   No ___

If yes, location:

Visitation: (Funeral home, church, home, other)

Preferred or suggested funeral or cremation service provider,

Location:

Transfer service, (If not to be provided by above service provider.)

_____

_____

Cemetery,

_____

_____

Location:

_____

_____

Clergy,

_____

_____

Cremated:

Type of urn:

_____

_____

Instructions for service,

_____

_____

_____

_____

_____

Buried:

Type of casket:

_____

_____

Open or closed casket? Open _____ Closed _____

Instructions for service, (In addition to all below)

_____

_____

_____

_____

_____

_____

Memorial service: (Instructions in addition to below, if body is donated, not present, etc.)

_____

_____

Headstone or monument:

_____

_____

Inscription/epitaph for headstone, or monument:

_____

Music selection for funeral and service:

_____

_____

_____

_____

Readings at funeral and service: (Hymns/Scriptures, poem, etc.)

_____

_____

_____

_____

Floral requests or donations in lieu of flowers?

_____

_____

_____

_____

Clothing and dressing requests:

_____

_____

_____

_____

Jewelry requests:

_____

Jewelry to be returned after service to estate trustee/executor to follow Will instructions?

_____

_____

Glasses On _____ Off _____

To be buried with you: Jewelry listed _____ Glasses _____

Items to be displayed: awards, trophies, crafts, specific photos, etc.

_____

_____

Organizations you would like notified: Company, school, troupe, band, lodge, society or fraternal organization

_____

_____

_____

_____

Notes or details to add to obituary: (Besides below)

_____

_____

_____

_____

_____

_____

Obituary to be published in the following:

_____

_____

Place of birth

_____

Date of birth   _____

Married   _____

Wedding date   _____

Religious affiliation

_____

Clubs, lodges, etc.

_____

Military service / war record

_____

Information about employment

_____

_____

Spouse, widow or widower of

_____

Date of death of spouse

_____

Children and residence

_____

_____

_____

_____

Grandchildren and residence

_____

_____

_____

_____

Siblings and residence

_____

_____

_____

_____

Pall Bearer's Names:

_____

_____

_____

_____

_____

_____

_____

_____

Honorary Pall Bearer's

_____

_____

_____

_____

_____

_____

_____

Other notes related to wishes, beliefs, processes, rituals, culture, details, etc.:

_____

_____

_____

_____

_____

_____

_____

_____

_____

_____

_____

_____

i) Body or Organ Donation

I wish to include the following wishes and/or have them be known in a memorandum.

I would like to donate:

Full body   Yes _____ No _____

All organs   Yes _____ No _____

Other detailed below: Yes _____ No _____

Notes:

_____

_____

If you wish to express in more detail your wishes related to your choice above.

i.e. Full body to a university or medical research institution

i.e. Only these organs, heart, lungs, liver, etc.

i.e. Only my eyes to an eye bank

i.e. All organs but not remaining tissue

_____

_____

_____

_____

_____

_____

_____

_____

_____

j) Instructions for Personal Care and Property

Fill in as much detail in each area with your wishes and notes. Refer back to the appropriate chapter when you need to review terms.

i) Choose your Representatives

I would like to appoint the following as my representative(s) to make all **Personal Care** decisions if I become disabled or incapacitated and cannot make these decisions:

Name

_____

Phone Numbers

_____

Address

_____

Jointly   Yes ___ No ___   and/or Severally Yes ___ No ___

Name

_____

Phone Numbers

_____

Address

_____

I would like to appoint the following as my representative to make all **Property** and financial decisions if I become disabled or incapacitated and cannot make these decisions:

Name

Phone Numbers

_____

Address

_____

Jointly　　Yes ___　No ___　and/or Severally　Yes ___　No ___

Name

_____

Phone Numbers

_____

Address

_____

I would like to appoint the following as my **Alternate** representative to make all **Personal Care** decisions if I become disabled or incapacitated and cannot make these decisions:

Name

_____

Phone Numbers

_____

Address

_____

Jointly　　Yes ___　No ___　and/or Severally　Yes ___　No ___

Name

_____

Phone Numbers

_____

Address

_____

I would like to appoint the following as my **Alternate** representative to make all **Property** decisions if I become disabled or incapacitated and cannot make these decisions:

Name

_____

Phone Numbers

_____

Address

_____

Jointly   Yes ___ No ___ and/or Severally Yes ___ No ___

Name

_____

Phone Numbers

_____

Address

_____

Process for resolving disputes between joint representatives:

1. Require a mediator to find a resolution   Yes ___ No ___
2. Submit to appropriate court for a resolution   Yes ___ No ___

What has to be done to determine or substantiate your incapacity?

Physician's statement?   Yes ___ No ___

And/or:

_____

_____

_____

ii) Type(s) of Power of Attorney to be Requested:

a. General   Yes ____ No ____

    Notes: _____

_____

b. Limited   Yes ____ No ____

    Notes: _____

_____

c. Enduring(Continuing)   Yes ____ No ____

    Notes: _____

_____

d. Springing   Yes ____ No ____

    Notes: _____

---

iii) Personal Care Wishes/Directives

If someone has to make decisions for you on the following five items, what direction would you give them?

Personal care related to:

    1. Shelter

    Notes: _____

_____

    2. Nutrition

Notes: _____

_____

3. Hygiene

Notes: _____

_____

4. Clothing

Notes: _____

_____

5. Safety

Notes: _____

_____

Health Care Directives

A person can specify what actions should be taken for their health if they are no longer able to make decisions for themselves because of illness or incapacity.

A short coming of most health care directives is that it is completed before medical practitioners have explained relevant treatment and care options.

You have the option here to fill in the chart, fill in specific details below the chart, or both.

Enter (Y) for yes or (N) for no, for the treatment if your health is each of the items listed in column one, in the corresponding cell according to your wishes:

	CPR	Respirator	Dialysis	Life-saving Surgery	Blood Transfusion	Life-saving Antibiotics	Intubation	Pain Relief
Current Health								
Terminal Permanent Coma								
Terminal Illness								
Mild Stroke								
Moderate Stroke								
Severe Stroke								
Mild Dementia								
Moderate Dementia								
Severe Dementia								

Additional notes on these items:

(It may seem repetitive, however as much details as possible is recommended so that drafted documents can be clear on your wishes.)

Terminal Illness

If my condition is determined to be terminal and with no hope of recovery, this is how I feel about it or I would like the following wishes adhered to if possible:

Life Support:

_____

_____

Intubation:

_____

_____

CPR:

_____

_____

DNR:

_____

_____

Persistent Unconsciousness

If I am persistently unconscious with no hope of recovery, this is how I feel about it, or I would like the following wishes adhered to if possible:

Life Support:

_____

_____

Intubation:

_____

_____

CPR:

_____

_____

DNR:

_____

_____

Severe and Permanent Mental Impairment

If I am severely and permanently mentally impaired, this is how I feel about it, or I would like the following wishes adhered to if possible:

Life Support:

_____

_____

Intubation:

_____

_____

CPR:

_____

_____

DNR:

_____

_____

Comfort and Dignity

Include the following statement or similar in my Personal Care Authorization regarding behavior controlling drugs: Yes ___ No ___

"If I am suffering from one of the above-mentioned conditions and if my behaviour becomes violent or is otherwise degrading, I want my symptoms to be controlled with appropriate drugs, even if that would worsen my physical condition or shorten my life."

Include the following statement in my Personal Care Authorization regarding pain controlling drugs: Yes ___ No ___

"If I am suffering from one of the above mentioned conditions and I appear to be in pain, I want my symptoms to be controlled with appropriate drugs, even if that would worsen my physical condition or shorten my life."

Other Treatments

I have strong feelings about certain kinds of treatment I wish to express in my Personal Care Authorization:

_____

_____

_____

_____

Indicate consent or refusal to each of the following treatments:

Antibiotics:

Consent _____   Refuse _____   Do Not Specify _____

Blood Transfusion:

Consent _____   Refuse _____   Do Not Specify _____

Chemotherapy:

Consent _____   Refuse _____   Do Not Specify _____

Defibrillation (heart stimulation):

Consent _____   Refuse _____   Do Not Specify _____

Intravenous (IV) Therapy:

Consent _____   Refuse _____   Do Not Specify _____

Intubation:

Consent _____   Refuse _____   Do Not Specify _____

Kydney Dialysis:

Consent _____ Refuse _____ Do Not Specify _____

Radiation:

Consent _____ Refuse _____ Do Not Specify _____

Surgery:

Consent _____ Refuse _____ Do Not Specify _____

Other personal notes or details to add related to medical care:

_____

_____

_____

_____

_____

_____

_____

_____

_____

_____

_____

_____

_____

_____

_____

_____

iv) Personal Property Wishes/Directives

If person named above for property has to make decisions for you on the following, what direction would you give them?

On a one time specific transaction; (i.e. On a real estate transaction);

_____

_____

If you become incapacitated; (Or another specific event?)

_____

_____

Instructions on managing your property, financial assets and belongings;

_____

_____

_____

_____

_____

Instructions under a general power of attorney - your appointee for property named above can manage your real estate and investments (including selling, buying, mortgaging), pay your bills and expenses, file your tax returns, manage your business, and sign most documents for you.

_____

_____

_____

_____

End of workbook.

v) Personal Property Memorandum

(Example -Related to bequests and legacies after you pass. i.e.)

- Please list your specific bequests
- Give as much detail as possible to each item's description.
- You can refer to this memorandum(s) in your Will.

I bequeath the following items of tangible personal property to the persons named/beneficiaries listed below:

Name of item and description:

_____

_____

Bequest to:

_____

Name of item and description:

_____

_____

Bequest to:

_____

Signature: _____

vii) Cash Legacies:

(Example)

You may leave specific cash amounts to people or charities in your Will provided there will be cash available in the estate after taxes, expenses, etc.

Amount:

_____

Give to:

_____

Amount:

_____

Give to:

_____

Amount:

_____

Give to:

_____

Amount:

_____

Give to:

_____

Signature: _____